THE SECRET WORLD OF

Beetles

THE SECRET WORLD OF

Beetles

Malcolm Penny

Chicago, Illinois

Project Editors: Geoff Barker, Marta Segal Block, Jennifer Mattson, Kathryn Walker
Production Manager: Brian Suderski
Consultant: Michael Chinery and Laura Jesse
Illustrated by Stuart Lafford
Designed by Ian Winton
Picture research by Vashti Gwynn
Planned and produced by Discovery Books

Library of Congress Cataloging-in-Publication Data:
Penny, Malcolm.
  Beetles / Malcolm Penny.
     v. cm. -- (The secret world of)
Includes bibliographical references (p.   ).
Contents: Success story -- Variations and adaptations -- Food and drink
-- Senses and defenses -- Reproduction -- Beetle life cycles -- Beetles
save the world -- Beetles and people.
  ISBN 0-7398-7020-3 (lib. bdg. : hardcover)
  1. Beetles--Juvenile literature. [1. Beetles.] I. Title. II. Series.
  QL576.2.P45 2003
  595.76--dc21

                              2003002240

Printed and bound in the United States by Lake Book Manufacturing, Inc.
07 06 05 04 03
10 9 8 7 6 5 4 3 2 1

Acknowledgments
The publisher would like to thank the following for permission to reproduce photographs:
p.8 (top) Dietmar Nill/Okapia/Oxford Scientific Films; p.8 (bottom) Anthony Bannister/Natural History Photographic Agency; p.9, 15 Ken Preston-Mafham/Premaphotos Wildlife; p.10 David M. Dennis/Oxford Scientific Films; p.11 James H. Robinson/Oxford Scientific Films; p.13, 22 Stephen Dalton/Natural History Photographic Library; p.14 G.J. Cambridge/Natural History Photographic Agency; p.16 (top) Dr. Ivan Polunin/Natural History Photographic Agency; p.16 (bottom) Oxford Scientific Films; p.17, 19 Paulo De Oliveira/Oxford Scientific Films; p.20, 43 Michael Fogden/Oxford Scientific Films; p.21 Daniel Heuclin/Natural History Photographic Agency; p.23 Harold O. Palo Jr./Natural History Photographic Agency; p.24 Mark Bowler/Natural History Photographic Agency; p.26 Michael Chinery; p.27 Jane Burton/Bruce Coleman Collection; p.28 Tim Shepherd/Oxford Scientific Films; p.29, 31, 32, 42 Oxford Scientific Films; p.30 Donald Specker/AA/Oxford Scientific Films; p.33 Waina Cheng/Oxford Scientific Films; p.34 David M.Dennis/Oxford Scientific Films; p.35 David Fox/Oxford Scientific Films; p.36 John Downer/Oxford Scientific Films; p.37 James Carmichael Jr./Natural History Photographic Agency; p.38 Anthony Bannister/Natural History Photographic Agency; p.39 Brojan Brecelj/Corbis; p.40 Dr. Rod Preston-Mafham/Premaphotos Wildlife; p.41 ImageQuest 3-D/Natural History Photographic Agency.

Other acknowledgments
Cover: Petr Zabransky/Bruce Coleman Collection; background images: Corbis

Note to the Reader
Some words are shown in bold, **like this.** You can find out
what they mean by looking in the glossary.

Contents

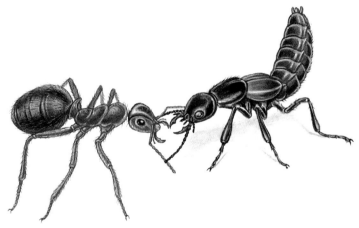

CHAPTER 1
Sturdy Survivors

 So far, about 370,000 species of beetle have been named.

 Scientists estimate that there may be as many as 5 million species of beetle still to be discovered.

 Some beetles bite people in self-defense, but none has a poisonous bite or a sting.

 Most adult insects, including beetles, live for less than a year, but some adult beetles live for a very long time. The oldest known adult beetle was a burying beetle that lived to be at least sixteen years old.

Beetles belong to the group of animals known as insects. Together with three other groups that include animals such as spiders, crabs, and centipedes, insects belong to a larger group of animals called **arthropods,** which means "jointed legs." All arthropods have a body that is covered by a hard outer layer called the **exoskeleton.** This is made up of plates with flexible joints between them.

Like other insects, beetles have six legs and a body that is divided into three sections: the head, the middle or **thorax,** and the **abdomen.** The head is equipped with eyes, **antennae,** short feelers around the mouth called **palps,** and mouthparts. Behind the head is the thorax, which contains the muscles that work two pairs of wings and three pairs of legs.

At the end of the beetle's body is the abdomen, which contains the internal organs. Beetles are different from other insects because their front wings, the **elytra** (or wing coverings), are hard. They fold down to cover the hind wings, meeting in a straight line down the middle of the back.

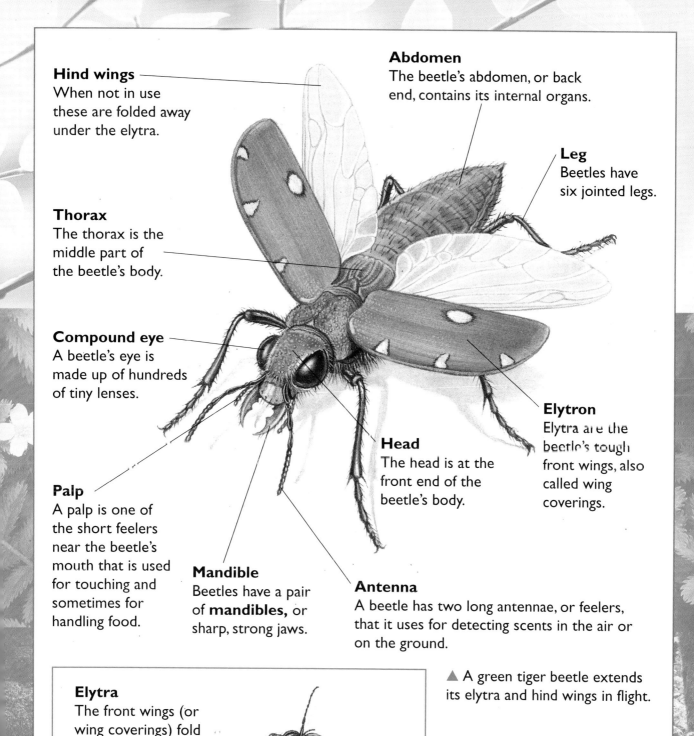

Hind wings
When not in use these are folded away under the elytra.

Abdomen
The beetle's abdomen, or back end, contains its internal organs.

Leg
Beetles have six jointed legs.

Thorax
The thorax is the middle part of the beetle's body.

Compound eye
A beetle's eye is made up of hundreds of tiny lenses.

Head
The head is at the front end of the beetle's body.

Elytron
Elytra are the beetle's tough front wings, also called wing coverings.

Palp
A palp is one of the short feelers near the beetle's mouth that is used for touching and sometimes for handling food.

Mandible
Beetles have a pair of **mandibles,** or sharp, strong jaws.

Antenna
A beetle has two long antennae, or feelers, that it uses for detecting scents in the air or on the ground.

Elytra
The front wings (or wing coverings) fold down to meet in a straight line.

▲ A green tiger beetle extends its elytra and hind wings in flight.

◀ When a beetle is not flying, the elytra form a hard, protective covering for the body and the more delicate hind wings.

ANCIENT ANCESTORS

The first beetles appeared about 300 million years ago, during the Devonian period—long before the dinosaurs. Dinosaurs did not appear until the beginning of the Triassic period, 225 million years ago, and they died out about 160 million years later. When *Tyrannosaurus rex* walked the earth, beetles were already an ancient form of life.

▲ This beetle fossil is about 150 million years old, but it looks similar to the beetles we see around us today.

A darkling beetle from the Namib Desert in Africa burrows headfirst into the sand.

A Giant Among Beetles

The size of a beetle is limited by the way it breathes. If a beetle grows too large it cannot draw in enough air to keep it alive through its **spiracles,** the tiny openings in its abdomen through which it breathes. Even so, the heaviest insect in the world is a beetle, the Goliath beetle from West Africa. It weighs between 2.5 and 3.5 ounces (70 and 100 grams) and is about 4.75 inches (120 millimeters) long.

SECRETS OF SUCCESS

There are several reasons beetles have existed for so long and in such great numbers. First, their very tough outer skeleton, or **exoskeleton,** and hard wing coverings allow them to **burrow** in loose soil and fallen leaves without getting injured. Second, beetles are able to withstand extremes of temperature and moisture levels. Above all, though, their bodies have adapted (changed over time) to survive almost anywhere on Earth and to feed on almost anything and everything.

CHAPTER 2
Variations and Adaptations

Beetles come in a large range of shapes, sizes, and colors, and they live in every **habitat** except the polar ice caps and the open ocean, though there are a few **species** that live along the shoreline.

All beetles were originally air-breathing land animals, but some evolved to be able to live in fresh or slightly salty water, including diving beetles and water scavenger beetles. The way organisms change to suit a particular way of life is called **adaptation.**

The smallest insects in the world are dwarf beetles, only 0.01 in. (0.25 mm) long.

The longest known beetle is the Hercules beetle of South and Central America, at more than 7.5 in. (190 mm).

A click beetle that is 0.5 in. (12 mm) long can launch itself nearly 1 ft (30 cm) into the air without using its legs.

Water beetles carry their air supply with them, trapped under their wing coverings.

The Eastern Hercules beetle is one of North America's largest beetles. The male of the species is easy to identify because of his long "horns."

HUNTERS

Ground beetles are the biggest family of **predatory** beetles. Most ground beetles live and search for food at night and hide under stones or logs during the day. Ground beetles have good eyesight, long legs to chase their **prey,** and powerful **mandibles** that they use to grab and kill prey.

The tiger beetle hunts prey by chasing after it and seizing it with its strong jaws.

Another predatory beetle, the tiger beetle, is nearly an inch (25 millimeters) long. It can run at more than 2 feet (60 centimeters) per second and will eat anything it can catch, mainly other insects and their young, including caterpillars.

11

Colorful lady beetles, also known as ladybugs, are a type of **predatory** beetle. They are rarely more than a quarter of an inch (6 millimeters) long and usually have a pattern of black spots on a red or yellow background. Both as wormlike **larvae** and as adults, lady beetles hunt bugs that eat plants, especially aphids.

Some ladybugs have yellow spots instead of black ones.

Long-horned beetles are named for their very long feelers.

Rove beetles belong to a very large family of mainly predatory beetles. They vary in size from less than half an inch to more than an inch (about 10 to 30 millimeters) long. Their wing cases are short, leaving most of their **abdomen** exposed.

The boll weevil's appetite for cotton bolls, or seed pods, makes it a threat to cotton crops.

SCAVENGERS

Many beetle families are **scavengers,** animals that eat dead remains or waste left behind by other animals. Scavengers are important because they help **decompose** matter. Burying beetles dig away the ground under the corpse of a mouse or bird until it sinks below the surface, where the beetles can feed on it as needed. Dung beetles eat animal droppings; other scavengers eat **fungi** that grow around rotting plants and animals.

BEETLES ON PLANTS

Many beetles and their larvae feed on leaves and often reduce them to spiky skeletons. For example, the Colorado potato beetle destroys potato leaves. Others, such as the rose chafer beetle, feed on pollen and nectar and nibble the petals of flowers. Some beetles found on flowers are actually lurking there to capture other insects. Many wood-eating beetles live in trees, **burrowing** into the trunks and spoiling the timber. Some of these beetles carry a type of fungus that can kill the trees.

This metallic green chafer beetle is often found on flowers because it feeds on leaves and petals.

WATER BEETLES

Crawling water beetles feed on plants that grow in ponds. They swim awkwardly, moving their legs as if they were walking. Sometimes they look as if they have fallen into the water accidentally. Diving beetles and water **scavengers** are much better swimmers. They move quickly underwater with sweeping strokes of their hind legs.

Whirligig beetles often swim in circles on the water's surface. They have special eyes, each of which is divided into two sections: one for seeing above water and the other for seeing below the surface.

The great diving beetle is a powerful swimmer with strong back legs that it uses like paddles. It is a fierce hunter that can even attack and kill small fish.

SPECIAL DIETS

Many beetles are very picky about what they eat. Weevils are tough beetles that often have long snouts for drilling into their food. However, each species of weevil typically feeds on only one type of food. Grain weevils eat stored wheat or other grains and are usually considered pests by humans. The most specialized

This big-footed weevil, common in rain forests, is perfectly suited to walking on slippery, wet leaves.

beetle in the world might be the beaver beetle. It lives only in the fur of living beavers and feeds on mites that suck the beaver's blood. Although the beetle spends much of its life underwater, it survives by breathing the air that gets trapped in the beaver's fur.

ODDITIES

The fireflies are a family of beetles whose **abdomens** light up when they are looking for a mating partner. In some **species** the female cannot fly but sits on the ground as she signals. In other species both males and females fly, producing flashes of light in a kind of code that is recognized by members of their own species.

▲ Fireflies produce light from organs in their abdomens without producing heat.

Click beetles have a unique way of escaping from trouble. If one is disturbed while on a plant, it will drop off, land on its back, and play dead. Later it will flex its body in a certain way to fling itself into the air, producing a loud click. Doing this usually lands the beetle right-side up.

Click beetles that have landed on their backs lie still to avoid being caught by an attacker. Then, when they are safe, they flip themselves over.

On the Wing

When most beetles fly, they hold their wing coverings out to the sides like the wings of an aircraft and move their hind wings. This long-horned beetle in flight shows how the wing coverings lift up so the hind wings can move freely. Only one group of beetles, which includes the rose chafer and the Goliath beetle, can fly with the wing coverings closed. These beetles have a special notch in each wing covering through which the hind wings can extend.

I DIDN'T KNOW THAT

CHAPTER 3
Food and Drink

Ground beetles are mainly hunters, but they also eat the unripe seeds of certain plants.

Some hunting larvae do not chew up their prey, but suck it dry the way that spiders do.

The larvae of furniture beetles do not need to drink water: they obtain all they need by breaking down fat in their bodies.

Large diving beetles often catch tadpoles or even small fish.

All beetles need food, especially **larvae** while they are growing and females as they are developing eggs. Different species have different ways of finding their meals. The larvae of the oil beetle, a member of the blister beetle family, climb up flowers and wait for a bee to visit. When a bee arrives, a larva hitches a ride back to the bee's nest. Once there, it molts into a differently shaped larva. Then it gradually eats the bees' eggs and pollen stores.

Some rove beetles also live in other insects' nests. Several **species** spend their adult lives in ants' nests, eating the eggs and larvae.

A rove beetle (right) asks an ant for food by tickling it with its antennae.

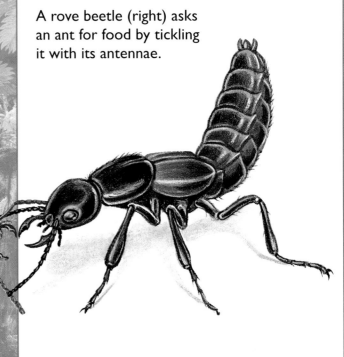

These rove beetles also beg for food by tickling the ants with their **antennae.** This is how the ants demand food from one another. When beetles use this signal, the ants give them whatever they are feeding to their fellow worker ants. When the beetle larvae hatch in the ants' nest, they eat the ants' larvae, but the ants do not drive them away. In fact, the ants want them to stay, because the beetles produce a sweet liquid from their **abdomen** that ants like to eat.

This species of ground beetle lives close to rivers and ponds. Here it uses its powerful jaws to feed on a water bug.

A CHANGE OF DIET

Ground beetles are mainly meat eaters, or carnivores, but in certain seasons their diet includes seeds, especially the soft, unripe seeds of plants such as wild chervil and wild carrots. One European ground beetle has an interesting diet in the summer: it eats the seeds on the skins of strawberries.

OUTSIDE DIGESTION

Like other animals, most beetles use their jaws to break their food into pieces small enough to swallow. Some **predatory** beetles do not chew up their **prey,** but crush it and pour **digestive juices** over it. They then suck out the fluids after the juices take effect. In this way, they can eat prey animals like slugs and snails that have rubbery outer skins and that are too big for the beetles to eat whole.

WATER

With a few exceptions, almost all beetles need water. They suck up

A darkling beetle from the Namib Desert in Africa tips itself so that dew that has collected on its body will flow into its mouth.

drops of water caught on leaves. Beetles that live in deserts have an advantage over other desert animals. They can trap moist air under their wing coverings in much the same way that water beetles trap air bubbles under their wing coverings to breathe underwater. Although trapping moisture protects desert beetles from drying up, they still must conserve water. They avoid the hot sun by coming out mostly at night.

Potato Plague

Many plants have poisons that protect them from being eaten by animals, but some beetles are able to resist the poison. For example, buffalo bur is a poisonous prairie plant, but the Colorado potato beetle can eat it without being harmed. When people began planting the prairies with potatoes, which belong to the same family of plants as the buffalo bur, Colorado potato beetles soon had a new favorite food. They are now a serious pest to potatoes all over the world.

I DIDN'T KNOW THAT

A species of darkling beetle from the Namib Desert in Africa has an unusual way of getting the water it needs. Its wing coverings have tiny bumps that trap droplets of water from fog. The water then trickles down into their mouths. Scientists are now developing ways for people to collect water from fog that are inspired by these beetles.

CHAPTER 4
Senses and Defenses

 Male beetles can detect females from miles away, using antennae covered in thousands of scent receptors.

 Blister beetles produce a chemical that causes painful blisters on human skin.

 Tiger beetles are the sprinters of the insect world. An Australian species can run up to 2.5 meters per second, or 125 body lengths per second. If a horse could run that quickly relative to its own body length, it would gallop at nearly 700 miles per hour!

 The colors of beetles can help hide them from their enemies or warn potential attackers that they are poisonous.

Like other insects, beetles have **compound eyes** made up of hundreds of light **receptors,** each of which produces its own tiny image. A beetle's view of the world may be something like watching numerous television screens showing slightly different pictures.

Predatory beetles can pounce on their **prey,** suggesting that they can judge distance quite well. However, beetles' main use of vision is probably to see danger coming so they can escape from it.

No one knows for sure what the world looks like to this harlequin beetle through its pair of compound eyes.

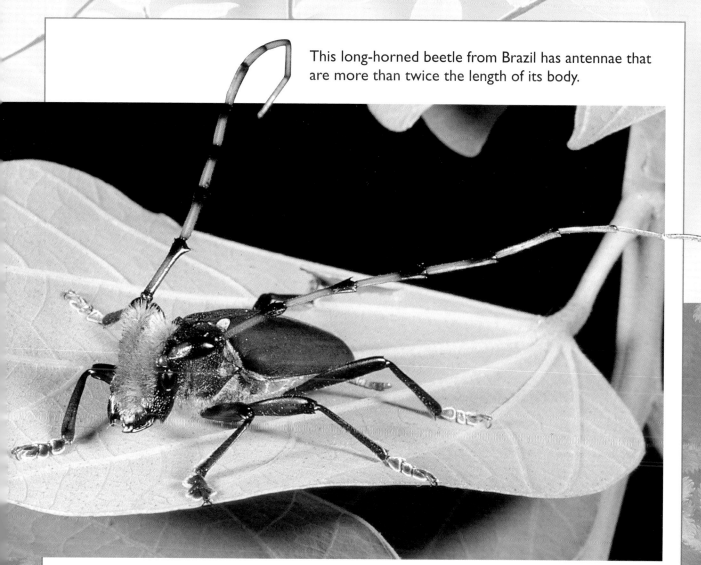

This long-horned beetle from Brazil has antennae that are more than twice the length of its body.

Scent is more important to beetles than sight. Both males and females use their **antennae,** which are covered in scent receptors, to find food. Males usually have much bigger antennae, often branched and feathery, with many thousands of receptors. The receptors are so sensitive that they can detect a single molecule of scent produced by a female miles away. Many male beetles find mates in this way.

Beetles do not have ears like those of grasshoppers and crickets, but they respond to some sounds, especially high-pitched tones. They sense them by feeling vibrations in the air through touch-sensitive hairs all over their body. The **palps** on the head are used mainly for touch, though some beetles use them to manipulate food when they are feeding. Bristles on their legs are also important touch organs.

A devil's coach horse scares off enemies by raising its tail, making it look like a scorpion.

EXPLODING BEETLES

The most dramatic beetle defense is that of the bombardier beetle, a type of ground beetle. It can eject a small cloud of vapor from the end of its **abdomen** with an audible popping sound. In some **species** the vapor is boiling hot. The puff of vapor frightens and temporarily blinds an attacker. The common American species of the bombardier beetle is only half an inch (12 millimeters) long, but the explosion it produces can still be alarming to a nearby animal.

The bombardier beetle produces chemicals from special glands in its abdomen. The chemicals explode when they are mixed.

DEFENSES

Beetles have various ways of defending themselves against would-be attackers. Some strike threatening poses when disturbed. A large European rove beetle known as the devil's coach horse, 1.25 inches (30 millimeters) long, raises its tail to look like a scorpion. Others, like lady beetles (ladybugs), play dead, folding their legs against their body. Some beetles produce bad-smelling or poisonous chemicals. Oil beetles release an oily, smelly substance from their joints that stings human skin. They are members of a larger family of beetles called blister beetles. All blister beetles produce the same stinging substance, which is called cantharidin.

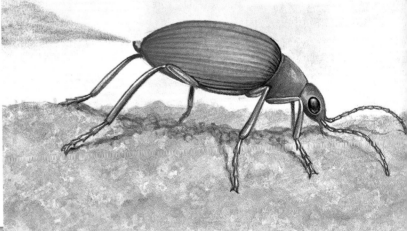

Useful Colors

Blister beetles in the United States are easy to spot. Some have black and orange stripes, while others are black with gray edges. Birds recognize these color patterns and avoid them. A burying beetle that lives in the eastern United States has yellowish orange stripes and makes a buzzing noise when threatened. **Predators** are likely to mistake it for a stinging bee and keep their distance. Most other species of beetle use colors as **camouflage** to make them more difficult for their enemies to see.

An Irresistible Perfume

Ambrosia beetles seek out freshly dead wood in old forests, following the scent of the alcohol that is produced when the soft inner bark first begins to rot. As they **burrow** into the wood, they release a scent that attracts beetles of the opposite sex from far away to mate with them.

CHAPTER 5
Reproduction

Diving beetles lay their eggs in plant stems that contain air. The wormlike larvae feed in the water, but move to the land when they are ready to become adults.

Each species of weevil usually lays its eggs on the leaves or in the fruits of one kind of plant.

The American burying beetle, an endangered species, is unusual among beetles because both parents participate in the care of the eggs and larvae.

Male beetles usually find mates by flying to follow the scent that the females produce. Some **species** find each other on foot, either by chance or by going to a certain place at the right time. Sometimes, however, the female goes in search of the male. A sky-blue European scarab beetle climbs a plant stem and waits for a female to arrive. The females are dull brown and live in the ground for most of the year, but at breeding time they climb plants until they find a male. After mating, the female drops to the ground and **burrows** into the soil to lay her eggs.

A sky-blue male scarab beetle waits to be discovered by a female.

WRESTLING MALES

Two European scarab males waiting for a female on the same stem will fight for the right to stay, each trying to throw the other off. Other beetles fight in the same way. Hercules beetles in South and Central America, or stag beetles in Europe and North America, lock horns and wrestle for as long as an hour before one backs down.

When stag beetles wrestle, the stronger male holds his opponent in the air until he stops struggling. Then the victorious male drops the loser to the ground.

It is very rare for either beetle to be hurt in these fights. Long-horned beetles cannot grip each other in the same way, so they push their heads together until the weaker one gives up.

LAYING EGGS

Like most other insects, all beetles lay eggs. Each beetle **species** has its own particular way of giving its eggs the best chance to develop and hatch. The weevils, a very large beetle family with more than 30,000 species worldwide (more than six times as many as all mammal species in the world), are particularly careful about where they lay their eggs.

The female hazel weevil uses her long snout to bore a hole into an unripe hazelnut, and she lays an egg into it. She then seals the hole with a drop of sticky fluid from her mouth. The egg hatches as the nut ripens, and the **larva** eats the nut from the inside out. Another weevil lays its eggs in the acorns that grow on oak trees. Others roll a cluster of eggs up inside a leaf, and still others lay one egg at a time inside the buds of fruit trees.

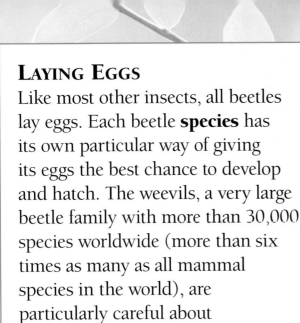

After mating, the female acorn weevil drills a hole through the shell of a developing acorn with her long snout. She then deposits her eggs in the acorn. When the larvae hatch, they use the inside of the nut as their food supply.

UNDERWATER EGGS

Some female water **scavenger** beetles have a special **adaptation** to prevent their eggs from getting too wet. Glands at the end of their **abdomen** produce a type of silk. The beetle wraps her eggs with the silk, making a waterproof packet that she then attaches to the bottom of a pond.

▶ The silver water beetle protects her eggs by wrapping them in a fluffy layer of silk.

Funnel to provide air for the eggs in case the raft sinks slightly underwater

Eggs inside silken case

Giant water scavenger beetles, which can be up to 2 inches (50 millimeters) long, take even greater care to protect their eggs. The female lays her eggs on a raft made of silk so that the eggs can float on the water. The raft is wrapped in a loose, fluffy layer of silk with a tall funnel at one end that provides air if the raft dips underwater.

The silken case of a water scavenger beetle is like a small boat. It keeps the eggs safe and dry and provides them with a supply of air.

29

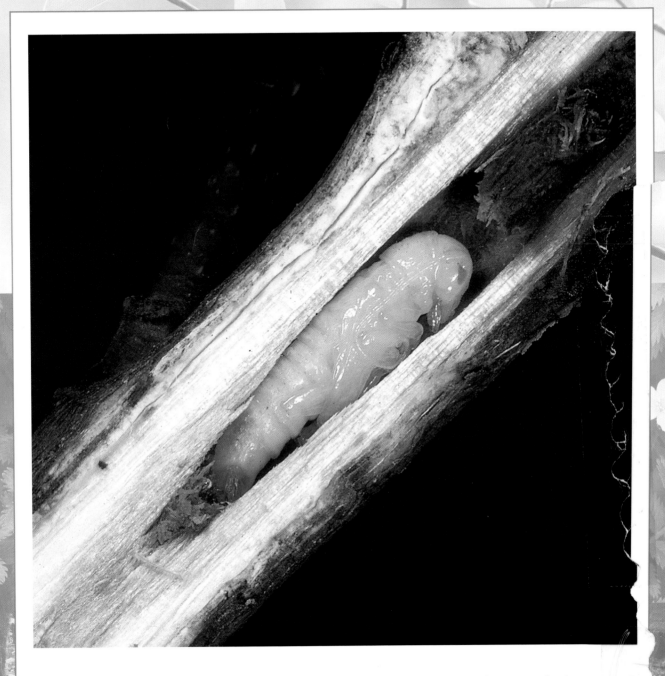

WOOD BORERS

Some beetles lay their eggs on or in dead wood. The female makes one or more passages in the wood and lays an egg in each one. When the **larva** hatches, it chews through the wood, making a tunnel behind it that fills up with its droppings.

A split in a poplar sapling reveals the pupa of a wood-boring beetle in the tunnel where it has developed.

Bark beetles lay eggs under the bark of logs and stumps, as well as on some living trees. Some of these beetles carry diseases that can kill the trees that they **burrow** into.

Deathwatch Beetles

The deathwatch beetle, a type of furniture beetle common in the United Kingdom, has a story behind its name. In the past, when someone was dying or had died, their friends and family used to stay awake all night in the house. This was called a deathwatch. The house would be so quiet that watchers could hear nighttime sounds that they usually missed. They could even hear beetles calling for mates by tapping their heads against their burrows in the house timbers.

EAT OR DIE

The poplar beetle cuts a U shape in the bark of an aspen tree and lays an egg in it. The tree grows a swelling, called a gall, where the beetle made the cut, and the larva eats the nutritious center of the gall. However, in a good growing season, the gall may grow more quickly than usual. This threatens to crush the larva, which then has to eat its way out or die.

CHAPTER 6
Beetle Life Cycles

One reason beetles have survived for so many millions of years is that they have two separate active stages to their lives. Because the two stages are so different, the adults and **larvae** do not compete for food or places to live. They spend the first of these active stages as wormlike larvae that hatch from the eggs. Adulthood is the second active stage.

A lady beetle larva helps out in a garden by eating an aphid, which eats plants.

Beetles have four stages in their life cycle: egg, larva, pupa, and adult. The pupa is an inactive stage during which the insect completely changes its form.

The life cycle of the beetle often takes more than a year. Some wood-feeding beetle larvae can live for 30 years before reaching adulthood.

The long-horned leaf beetle is the only beetle that changes into a pupa while underwater. Its pupae have tubes that connect them to the air channels of a plant.

PREDATORY LARVAE

The larvae of some beetles are **predators** as soon as they have hatched, though at first their **prey** is very small. Lady beetle (ladybug) larvae, for example, chase the same plant bugs that their parents eat, while tiger beetle larvae sit and wait for their food to come to them. A female tiger beetle lays an egg in a hole in the ground and covers it with soil. When the egg hatches, the larva lies face-up

A hungry tiger beetle larva stays at the top of its burrow with its head at the entrance. Its huge, flat head forms a kind of plug that hides the hole. The larva lies in wait for a passing insect, which it will then grasp with its powerful jaws.

at the entrance of the **burrow** with its jaws open. When a small creature walks across the opening, the larva grabs it and drags it into the tunnel to eat. As the larva grows, it digs the burrow deeper so that it has enough room.

UNDERGROUND LARVAE

Many beetles lay their eggs in the ground. When the white, wormlike **larvae** hatch, they **burrow** through the soil and eat the roots of plants. They grow very fat during the two or more years that they spend feeding in this way. The large, pale larvae of june bugs (also called chafers) and other large beetles are a favorite food of birds, which are very good at digging them out of the ground.

A RESTING PERIOD

When a larva is fully grown, it **pupates,** or turns into a **pupa.** This is the resting stage during which its body changes into that of an adult. It must find a sheltered place where the motionless pupa will not be exposed to **predators.** Beetle pupae have their legs free—unlike butterfly pupae, which are completely enclosed in a tough outer casing. After it has been a pupa for a certain period of time, the beetle will be ready to emerge as an adult.

The plump, white larvae of june bugs (chafers) can cause damage in the garden because they eat the roots of plants.

LIFE CYCLE OF A TIGER BEETLE

1. The female makes a small burrow in the soil, and then lays a single egg in it. 2. The newly hatched larva tunnels to the surface, where it waits for passing prey. 3. The larva makes a small chamber and plugs the burrow with soil. Inside this chamber it enters the pupal stage. 4. The adult beetle emerges from the pupa. Then, after a rest period, it comes out of its burrow.

1.

2.

3.

4.

Pale Tiger

Tiger beetle pupae turn into adults in the fall, but then spend the winter underground waiting to emerge in the following spring. When they first emerge from the pupa stage, they are white, but they gradually take on the bright colors of an adult as the winter months go by.

35

CHAPTER 7
Helpful Beetles

Animal droppings, or dung, make good fertilizer for soil, but you can have too much of it. The world's grasslands, such as the American prairies, where millions of buffalo once roamed, or the African plains where millions of antelope graze, would be buried many feet deep in their droppings—if it were not for the activities of the dung beetles. Dung beetles eat animal droppings, but some also bury enormous quantities every breeding season to feed their growing **larvae.**

By burying any dung (droppings) that they find, dung beetles add nutrients to the soil and improve the quality of the grass for grazing animals.

The family of dung beetles includes some of the biggest of all beetles.

Some dung beetles dig burrows that are nearly 5 ft (1.5 m) deep.

Drivers in open vehicles in Africa sometimes wear helmets and goggles at night, to protect them from being hit by flying beetles.

A herd of wildebeests grazing on the grassy plains of the Serengeti in Tanzania, Africa. If not for beetles, the animals' dung would cover the landscape.

ABOVE AND BELOW GROUND

Dung beetles primarily use dung as a place for the female to lay her eggs. In **species** of beetle that breed in this way, the male dies soon after mating and the female guards the eggs until they hatch

Some species dig a deep **burrow** to bury the dung. The female does most of the work, while the male clears away the soil and gathers

Dung beetles can be amazingly colorful. This gleaming species lives in Florida.

dung. The larvae usually feed for about a month and spend two weeks as **pupae** before emerging as adults. Some larger larvae take much longer to emerge. Their parents keep bringing fresh dung for them until they **pupate,** which might take as long as two years.

THE BALL ROLLERS

African scarab beetles have a more complex system of using dung. They are known as ball rollers, because the male gathers dung into a ball with his legs and his shovel-shaped head and jaws, and then he rolls it away with his long hind legs. The ball can be several times heavier than the beetle. In large **species** it might even be as large as a tennis ball. In some species the females help to push it, while in others they just hitch a ride on the ball. On the way to the breeding place, other males often fight fiercely to take over the ball. When the pair reaches the chosen place, usually somewhere with light, sandy soil, the male pushes soil away from beneath the ball until it sinks into the ground. Once the ball has been buried, the female digs a series of chambers beside it in which she lays her eggs.

In this species of ball-rolling beetle, both partners help to roll away a ball toward their chosen nesting place.

Underworld Guardians

The ancient Egyptians were very familiar with dung beetles. They associated the ball of dung sinking into the ground with the setting of the sun, disappearing only to rise again. They thought that the beetles died when they went underground to lay their eggs, and then came back to life when the new adults emerged. Egyptians buried their dead with carved scarab beetles to guard them in the underworld.

DUNG BEETLES IN DANGER

In some parts of the world, dung beetles are under threat. Cattle today are given so many drugs to keep them free of diseases that their dung is almost sterile. This means that it no longer contains the **microorganisms** that beetle **larvae** feed on. This is a problem for the beetles, but also for farmers—and for the rest of us, who depend on the food farmers grow. Without beetles, disposing of dung could become a serious problem.

CHAPTER 8
Beetles and People

Many different **species** of beetle are helpful to people. While dung beetles keep the ground clear of animal droppings, and burying beetles dispose of dead animals, other beetles help gardeners and farmers by controlling pests. Ground beetles eat the slugs and caterpillars that ruin many crops, and rove beetles eat many other types of **larvae** and adult insects considered pests. Lady beetles (ladybugs) eat sap-sucking aphids. Many people buy lady beetles to release into their gardens.

Adult ladybugs are just as good at hunting aphids as they were when they were larvae.

A single female lady beetle (ladybug) can produce enough young in one season to eat 200,000 aphids.

Beetles help many plants and flowers by carrying pollen from one flower to another.

Boll weevils, which had made it impossible to grow cotton in Mexico by 1863, entered the United States in 1892 and became a pest to cotton here.

Grain weevils can completely destroy stored wheat, leaving nothing but empty husks.

However, beetles are under threat in many parts of the world. Nine species of beetle in the United States are classified as threatened or endangered, including the American burying beetle.

THE PESTS

One of the reasons for this is that many beetles cause problems for people. Weevils are among the main enemies of people who grow and store food. The boll weevil, a beetle that lives on the seed pods (called bolls) of cotton plants, has threatened the cotton crop in the southern United States since the end of the 1800s. But long before then, the ancient Egyptians had problems with grain weevils, and weevil wing coverings have been found in the remains of ancient Roman food stores.

The larvae of powderpost beetles do real damage to house timbers and furniture as they eat their way to adulthood. Some kinds of beetle larvae eat carpets and curtains, and the leather bindings of old, rare books. There is even a beetle that specializes in invading museums; in fact, it often feeds on collections of dead beetles.

Pest Controllers

A **species** of rove beetle introduced to the United States from Europe kills cabbage root fly maggots, a serious pest of plants such as cabbages, radishes, and broccoli. The beetle **larvae** live in and kill the fly **pupae,** while the adults eat both eggs and maggots. During their lifetime, one pair of beetles may destroy 1,200 eggs and 130 maggots, as well as hundreds of fly pupae.

WAR ON BEETLES

Humans have invented pesticides to kill beetles as well as coatings for seeds to protect them from attacks. Unfortunately, a spray aimed at one kind of pest beetle also kills any other insects that it contacts. These include helpful ones, such as lady beetles that hunt aphids and ground beetles that eat the caterpillars of codling moths, which **burrow** into fruit and can ruin a crop. Some pesticides can be dangerous to people as well.

BETTER METHODS

Scientists have been studying ways of controlling particular species instead of just killing all the insects that live in a crop. They have developed one such method that uses traps baited with the scent produced by a female looking for a mate. This type of trap will draw in only males of the targeted species, because each species has its own special scent. Boll weevils can be controlled by a method sometimes called clean cropping, in which all the dead and diseased bolls containing the **pupae** are cut off and burned so that the weevil population is brought to a stop.

This gleaming silver beetle from the cloud forests of Costa Rica is just one of the beautiful and unique creatures found in tropical rain forests.

BEETLES FOREVER

More than 25 percent of all known animal species are beetles, and humans have probably discovered and named only a small fraction of all the beetles that exist. Although some beetles are unpopular with humans, the vast majority of them are harmless or helpful. It is only fair that these ancient and often quite beautiful creatures have a place in a world in which they have lived since before the dinosaurs existed.

Glossary

abdomen back section of an insect that contains the internal organs

adaptation characteristic developed by an organism over a long period of time that enables it to survive in a certain environment

antenna (more than one are called antennae) feelers on an insect's head used for touching and detecting tastes, smells, and sounds

arthropod member of one of the major groups of animals without backbones. Arthropods have a jointed outer skeleton and jointed legs.

burrow to dig a hole or tunnel. A hole or tunnel used by an animal as a home is also called a burrow.

camouflage color, shape, or pattern that disguises an animal by causing it to blend in with its background

compound eye eye made up of many tiny lenses and found mainly in adult insects

decompose to break down dead plants and animals. An organism that does this is often called a decomposer.

digestive juices acids produced in an organism's body to break down food that it has eaten or is about to eat

elytron (more than one are called elytra) one of a pair of hard front wings on a beetle's body. They are also called wing coverings.

exoskeleton hard outer skeleton of arthropods

fungus (more than one are called fungi) plantlike organism that does not produce its own food but feeds on dead plant and animal matter

habitat specific place where an organism lives

larva (more than one are called larvae) second, wormlike stage in the life cycle of most insects, after the egg and before the pupa

mandible one of a pair of insect mouthparts that are used as jaws

microorganism organism too small to be seen without a microscope

palp sensitive feeler near an insect's mouth that is used for handling food

predator animal that hunts other animals for food

predatory surviving by hunting and killing other animals to eat

prey animal that is hunted by other animals for food

pupa (more than one are called pupae) third stage in the life cycle of most insects in which the young insect develops into the adult form, usually inside a hard protective case. To pupate is to turn into a pupa.

receptor sensitive cell that detects certain kinds of information in an organism's surroundings, such as sounds, tastes, or sensations

scavenger animal that survives by eating other animals' wastes or leftovers, or the remains of dead animals

species group of organisms that share certain features and that can breed together to produce offspring that can also breed

spiracle tiny opening in an insect's body through which it breathes air

thorax middle part of an insect's body that contains muscles that move the wings and legs

Further Reading

Evans, Arthur V., and Charles L. Bellamy. *An Inordinate Fondness for Beetles*. Photographs by Lisa Charles Watson. New York: Holt, 1996.

Greenaway, Theresa. *Minipets: Beetles*. Chicago: Raintree, 1999.

McEvey, Shane. *Beetles*. Broomall, Penn.: Chelsea House, 2001.

Pascoe, Elaine. *Nature Close-Up: Beetles*. Photographs by Dwight Kuhn. Farmington Hills, Mich.: Blackbirch Press, 2001.

Sabuda, Robert, and Matthew Reinhart. *Young Naturalist's Pop-Up Handbook: Beetles*. New York: Hyperion, 2001.

Swan Miller, Sara. *Beetles: The Most Common Insects*. Danbury, Conn.: Franklin Watts, 2000.

Index

Numbers in *italic* indicate pictures